A Fair Is Fun

by Alice Tu

Reading Consultant: Wiley Blevins, M.A.
Phonics/Early Reading Specialist

 COMPASS POINT BOOKS

Minneapolis, Minnesota

Compass Point Books
3109 West 50th Street, #115
Minneapolis, MN 55410

Visit Compass Point Books on the Internet at *www.compasspointbooks.com*
or e-mail your request to *custserv@compasspointbooks.com*

Photographs ©: Cover and p. 1: Steve Pope Photography/Steve Pope, p. 6: Kip Malone
Photography, p. 7: USDA/Gordon Baer, p. 8: Corbis/Robert Holmes, p. 9: Corbis/Mug Shots,
p. 10: Steve Pope Photography/Steve Pope, p. 11: Corbis/Philip Gould, p. 12: Astro Amusement
Company/All Star Amusement Company/Thebault-Blomsness, Inc.

Editorial Development: Alice Dickstein, Alice Boynton
Photo Researcher: Wanda Winch
Design/Page Production: Silver Editions, Inc.

Library of Congress Cataloging-in-Publication Data
Tu, Alice.
    A fair is fun / by Alice Tu.
        p. cm. — (Compass Point phonics readers)
    Summary: Discusses a visit to a fair in an easy-to-read text that
incorporates phonics instruction and rebuses.
    ISBN 0-7565-0501-1 (hardcover : alk. paper)
    1. Agricultural exhibitions—Juvenile literature. 2. Fairs—Juvenile
literature. [1. Agricultural exhibitions. 2. Fairs. 3. Reading—Phonetic
method. 4. Rebuses.] I. Title. II. Series.
    S552.5.T8 2003
    394'.6—dc21   2003006345

Table of Contents

Dear Parent or Caregiver,

Welcome to Compass Point Phonics Readers, books of information for young children. Each book concentrates on specific phonic sounds and words commonly found in beginning reading materials. Featuring eye-catching photographs, every book explores a single science or social studies concept that is sure to grab a child's interest.

So snuggle up with your child, and let's begin. Start by reading aloud the Mother Goose nursery rhyme on the next page. As you read, stress the words in dark type. These are the words that contain the phonic sounds featured in this book. After several readings, pause before the rhyming words, and let your child chime in.

Now let's read *A Fair Is Fun*. If your child is a beginning reader, have him or her first read it silently. Then ask your child to read it aloud. For children who are not yet reading, read the book aloud as you run your finger under the words. Ask your child to imitate, or "echo," what he or she has just heard.

Discussing the book's content with your child:
Explain to your child that a state fair is an example of a community tradition. It is an event that takes place year after year. It celebrates the accomplishments of individuals. It also celebrates the different cultures in the community with music, dance, arts and crafts, and foods.

At the back of the book is a fun Nice Going! game. Your child will take pride in demonstrating his or her mastery of the phonic sounds and the high-frequency words.

Enjoy Compass Point Phonics Readers and watch your child read and learn!

Little Jack Horner

Little Jack Horner
Sat in the corner,
Eating his Christmas pie.
He put in his **thumb,**
And pulled out a **plum,**
And said, "What a good boy am I!"

It is a fair!
It is a lot of fun.

 jump and run fast.
They tug and tug, too.

 People stop and see a big pig.
Ted is proud of his pig.

Sam can jump and spin.
He has fun.

Ann makes red jam.
She wins a  ribbon.

Smell the  corn .
Stop at a snack stand. Yum!

The sun has set.
The fair ends until next year.

Word List

Short *u*
fun
jump
run
sun
tug
yum

s-Blends
fast
smell
snack
spin
stand
stop

High-Frequency
of
she
they
too

Social Studies
fair
proud
year

Nice Going!

Player 1

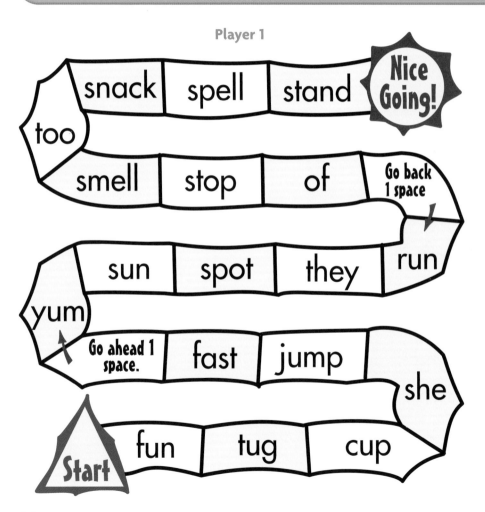

14

How to Play

- Each player puts a moving piece on his or her Start. Players take turns shaking the penny and dropping it on the table. Heads means move 1 space. Tails means move 2 spaces.
- The player moves and reads the word in the space. If the child cannot read the word, tell him or her what it is. On the next turn, the child must read the word before moving.
- If a player lands on a space having special directions, he or she should move accordingly.
- The first player to reach the *Nice Going!* sign wins the game.

Player 2

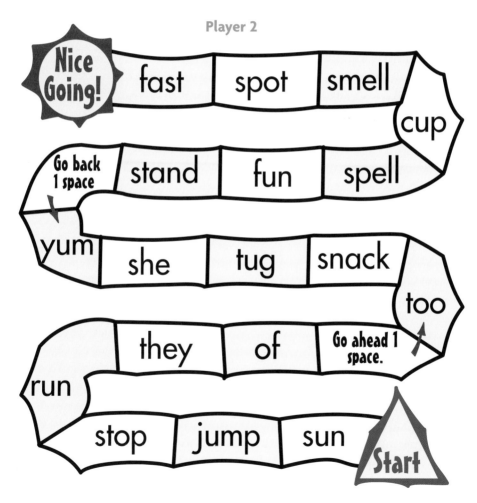

Read More

Ansary, Mir Tamim. *Southwest Indians*. Des Plaines, Ill.: Heinemann Library, 2000.

Bell, Rachel. *Pigs*. Chicago, Ill.: Heinemann Library, 2000.

Hall, Margaret. *Festivals*. Chicago, Ill.: Heinemann Library, 2002.

Wade, Mary Dodson. *Cinco de Mayo*. New York: Children's Press, 2003.

Index